I Wear the Colour Green

By Cedric L. Jones

PublishAmerica
Baltimore

First printing

PublishAmerica has allowed this work to remain exactly as the author intended, verbatim, without editorial input.

ISBN: 1-60563-317-8
PUBLISHED BY PUBLISHAMERICA, LLLP
www.publishamerica.com
Baltimore

Printed in the United States of America

For Kimberly Ann Cook.
It does get greater later.

Part One

From the Mind

Searching

Someone whispers softly
Of a tale that has been told.
My heart fills with wet sorrow,
My hands release their hold.

My mind delves deep through time,
Grasping not, it roams.
I choke the tears I find,
Still I search for home.

When the darkness breaks away,
I take your hand in mine.
We step forward through the looking glass,
Onward lost in time.

Parted in our path,
Alone, and left behind,
I break away and onward go,
Searching, yet to find.

The Lazy Days of Summer

Close your eyes and drift with me
Past rain and wind and thunder,
Through the angels' breeze to the mermaids' seas
On the lazy days of summer.

Where castles rise against the skies
And beauty is a hunter,
And butterflies the carpets ride
On the lazy days of summer.

Where clouds are high, the grasses grow
And sleep becomes a wonder,
Where people pass and smile as they go
On the lazy days of summer.

Where fairies dance and flowers grow
To the rat-a-tat of nature's drummer,
And worries go, and lovers know
The lazy days of summer.

The Innocent Wise

The view of the world from my eyes
Is the view of the world from a child's,
A purity so soft and sweet,
An innocence so mild.

"Look to the children for answers," they said,
"And answers the children will give."
The answers divinity sends from above,
A guide to how we should live.

"Give to the children a dream," they said,
"In reality the dream will come true."
Give to them love, and in love they shall grow,
For there's nothing a child cannot do.

Blessed be our children,
For our children do love us so.
The powers that be know the theme of my song,
While my child knows the path I must go.

Runaway Child

Stop!
Before you take that step
And think
While tilting on the brink
Of now and forever.
Think about the future,
Where you'll wind up if you stay.
Think about your life
Where you'll wind up if you leave.
Nothing is as permanent
As a childhood gone too wrong.
So, run away child
Into music, into song.
In your imagination waits
A symphony so long
It lasts you through the sad days
When everything seems wrong.
Run into a book.
Where they won't think to look.
Have adventure, have a journey
Have chaos in the wind
Until the end.
And on that day you can escape,
You'll be glad you didn't take
That unknown path.
Then, in ten years
You'll look back
And realize that you did lack
The strength to face the long dark street

That opened up its mouth to eat a
Runaway Child.
Take a deep breath,
Close that door.
I won't lecture you no more.
I can't tell you what you should do anyway.
All I know is what I know,
Be prepared before you go.
That's what I decided
My own fateful day.

In the Mist

As the mist caresses the highway,
We drive right into it.
Some call it fog.
I call it the future,
The future that is hidden from us.
Some ignore it.
I move into it.
I see what will be…and what I want to be.
Some fight fate.
I am satisfied; I like what I see.
I ain't no fortuneteller, palmist or crystal gazer.
I am a mist dweller.
I strive for the future.
It says so…in the mist.

Couples

And I spy,
Sitting beneath the stars, embraced,
Moon on their shoulders, bathing tenderly,
Night air soft on their skins,
Night songs singing in their ears,
Grass cool beneath their bodies,
Thoughts pure inside their heads,
Words blown upon their lips,
Lights blazed within their eyes.
Alive,
Couples.

And I'm Alone

Must I feel so alone
In a world so full of souls?
My cry receives no answer.
I need someone to hear.
I reach for taunting figures,
Shadows
Gone and I'm alone.

Forever weeping silently
Tears that are not real.
Hearts are marble cold.
I find no warmth for me.
I pray and pine embrace
But marble breaks
And I'm alone.

I hear the songs of angels.
I look, they wash away.
Mournful of my plight,
I leave my roads diverged.
I hide my dreams from light
To be alas, a child, abashed,
Alive alone.

What Is Love?

I search the world over
Looking for a dream.
Day by day I'm older,
And I feel
Can it all be over?
Is life what it seems?
I turn surely colder
Wondering.

What is love
In this world so full of souls?
What is love,
Can I find it as of old?
I sit alone and wonder.
I ask help of God above.
But still I need an answer,
What is love?

I walk the street at night
Wiping tears from my face.
I'm looking for my light
In the dark.
The night turns into daylight,
And I'm yet without a place.
My question burns a path right
Through my heart.

What is love,
And why am I so all alone?
What is love—
Will I ever find my own?
I pray to find an answer,
But I can never learn enough.
I'm alone at night and I wonder,
What is love?

What is love
In this world so full of souls?
What is love—
Will I ever find my own?
I know someone is waiting,
But I shed tears when times are tough.
Someday I know, I'll know
What is love.

I Still Keep Holding On

I look outside the window
And I see reality.
I go to sleep and dream,
But no one dreams of me.
I long to be with someone,
But I face the night alone.
The silence is so real
And the stars, they know my song.

And I imagine
That there's some place, some time, somewhere
That I belong.
And, no matter what,
I still keep holding on.

I fly on golden wings
But in morning I awake.
Sometimes they seem so real,
These fantasies I make.
I long to be with someone,
But that never comes true.
And I'll never see a different world,
No matter what I do.

And I imagine
That there's some place, some time, somewhere
That I belong.
And, no matter what,
I still keep holding on.

Do you ever wonder—
Wonder how I feel?
These tears I cry,
They fall and they are real.
And 'though I walk alone,
I still sing my song
And, no matter what,
I still keep holding on.

Yes, I imagine
That there's some place, some time, somewhere
That I belong.
And, no matter what,
I still keep holding on.

The Singer and the Song

The memory of you lingers fresh
And I see you in my mind.
I long to have you near again.
For your song, I pine.

Melodious, soft, sweet,
Angelic to the chord,
Intensity and brilliance
And love...and peace...and more.

Lifting, Pounding, Gripping, Sounding!
Coursing through my veins!
Then breathless, waiting, pleading, fading...
Never to know me again.

A teardrop swells upon my eye,
As I picture you as then.
And I pray to the gods the day will come
When we make music once again.

Broken

When a lonely heart is broken
And a smile no longer shines,
The laughter slowly dies
And the fervor melts inside.

When the moment is suddenly broken,
And all dreams are set askew,
My soul turns shades of blue
And my tears burn silent for you.

Then life is set asunder
And the day no longer fades,
But it shatters like a crystal,
And the shards bring tears of pain.

When a lonely heart is broken,
Yet, no one seems to care,
I'll cry about my broken heart,
And broken hearts everywhere.

Truth

Mommy we have lied to me.
I am not what you see.
Your mommy heart
Has blotted out the truth.

But man sees bitter strong
And he sees the beast in me
As I snarl at him
And bare my bloodied tooth.

As I pine mommy lullabies
I am driven to the dirt
Where glass and rubble
Grind my blood and bone.

Bastard born I, weary,
Roam the pathway evermore.
Yet, I'll never find the peace
They call home.

So sing sweet songs so sullenly
As my head rests on your heart
And my whole soul prays
What you sing is real.

My tears drain, as do ages pass,
And Mommy, I'm so old.
All that's left for me to do
Is feel.

Pillowhead

Pillowhead
Burned a lord called justice
In my yard,
Chanted hatred songs,
Danced with tall
Black guns.
Granny said he came before
And took away her home.
The burning lord had walked
Across the ground.
Pillowhead just laughed
And marched and burned.
He told us:
"You will never leave the dirt!"
We did and hovered
Because he could not always
Shoot us down.
Now, outside my door,
Pillowhead stands.
History is not yet in the past.
I tremble as I cock my gun
And wait.

History

I pricked my finger,
Out spilled blood.
Thickening history ran
Massahs and missus
And cotton,
On which I wiped
The dripping blood and read
The pages full.
The back doors
Of the alley ways
Swing segregated freedom,
Different water,
Different air,
Different jobs—
In court a separate Bible.
In church a separate God.
My God said be gentle,
His God said be fierce.
White cape, rope in hand.
A structure crackles deep in flames,
Deep in flames.
The massahs and missus are gone now,
Only a couple to spare.
Yet, in my blood
I'm toting on.
I feel the wounds,
But looking back will
Salt them even more.
Dripping blood
Reality
Can lock the alley doors.

Asphalt Fruit

The asphalt gardens bear
Strange fruit in the
Winter time,
Huddled alone
In darkened alleys,
Praying for kindness.
The sickly sweet, pungent
Aroma of neglect rises
To untrained nostrils
As we hurry home to
The warmth
Of our sheltered lives
And away from the fruit
Of an overgrown society.

Round and Round

Sadness is silence
When nothing stirs
But a bump and a grunt
And a click and a whir—
Cold steel pressed against your head.
If you wake up tomorrow
You'll wake up dead,
Robbed and beaten,
Raped and eaten
Up with rage
For a cage of fear
And the dangers near,
When cops and robbers
Shoot it out
While the world
Still calmly spins about,
Round and round and
Round and round
To glory.

We Live in Numbered Days

Half-a-mile across the world
We find ourselves in shame.
We've altered all the beauty,
And only War's to blame.

And through the years, our hearts may yell,
"A necessary cause!"
But after years of casualties,
We bring ourselves to pause.

We think of Heaven's children
That have lived their nation's fight.
They fought because what's wrong is wrong
And the nation's always right.

In uniforms of moss
They stalk the angry blood of man.
If they are killed, it's glorious
For, behind the flag they stand.

Consider carefully, my peers
The violence that we crave.
Then we realize, in truth,
We live in numbered days.

Moon Song

Silvery moon
Tell me what you see
High above the world
Blazing.
Crickets moan, people pass,
I wonder if they care
Why I sit alone
Wishing on the moon.
Even in the sun
I am alone.
Sunset and cold come
With the moon.
The marble steps are frigid
And the shadows thicken deep,
But the moon is overhead
Guarding.
If I die tonight,
Will you remain intact?
Or crumble or fall
Or flicker or wane?
And when I cry tonight,
Soak up my tears,
Hold me closer in your arms.
Or am I here alone
Singing moon songs?

Contemplating Suicide

Contemplating suicide.
My tears no longer fall.
My days are empty valentines,
So I run to be alone.

Contemplating suicide.
The voices fill my head.
The doors that close will lock themselves.
I fall asleep alone.

Contemplating suicide.
The sun burns evermore.
One less man to walk the earth.
One more dream deferred.

Contemplating suicide.
But they all hold on so fast.
They hold me close, and I am weak,
'Though I fight to be strong.

Contemplating suicide
I surrender to their care.
They make me see that life is light.
In the darkness, I'd be scared.

Contemplating suicide.
One day, I'll find my door.
So, I fall asleep and dream at night
And contemplate no more.

Friendship Eternal

When the wings of time have brushed us,
And somehow have drawn us apart,
We may come again together
In the spirit and in the heart.

And when distance is a constant reminder,
We may turn back the wheels of our minds
And remember our days of youth clearly
As lived for the very first time.

We may pray to again hear the laughter
As we once heard it many years before,
That the closeness and warmth that we're after
Make ageless our yearning for more.

So I write this verse in the present
So the future will bring back the past,
And as words live on, so will memory,
And in memory, our friendship shall last.

White Cat

A white cat crossed my path tonight,
Its eyes were full of light.
It leaped and trotted gracefully,
Then bounded out of sight.

It took away the troubles
That were resting on my mind.
It carried them upon its fur
And laid them down to lie.

It ran, then turned to look at me,
And ran on further still.
Its eyes were sharp beneath the night
And I listened to their will.

They seemed to beckon me to come
And follow through the night.
But I chose no, to keep my path,
And walked onward toward the light.

Once again, our night eyes locked.
I could hear its distant purr.
But as I said, it stole away,
And I saw the cat no more.

Green

And I wear the colour Green.
The colour hides my shades.
The leaves begin to tremble,
Deep within.

The Green drapes over lightly.
The colour Green wears me,
While the breeze rustles the garment
From within.

When I wear the Green in shadows,
It glows with eerie light
And the other colours brush
Against the folds.

'Though I stash the colour Green
'Neath crimson and 'neath gold,
The hues burst forth to sight
Out from within.

So I am the colour Green,
Wearing nature's crown,
And I spill forth the Green,
And take the Green
Within.

Study War No More

Dr. King is watching me.
His booming voice is ringing,
And I can hear the words.
I too dream, Doctor.
My dreams are not as great.
I dream to simply make it
In the world.
But never could I make it
If you had not lead the march.
So rest a while,
And we'll pick up the task.
Just rest your weary feet.
We've come along aways.
Like Lot's wife,
There is no turning back.
So we'll march on to Glory,
'Til we reach great Heaven's door
And sing it loud:
"Gon' study war no more!"

Freedom Song

Hand in hand we're
Walking toward tomorrow
Defying history and all its wrongs.
Tiny voices rise
In happy sorrow.
This is how we sing our freedom song.

Thank you God for bringing us together.
The rainbow that for all
These years we've longed.
We are the children
That will make forever
And this is how we sing our freedom song.

War does not bring laughter
To our faces.
Hate does not paint smiles
Across our hearts.
Peace breeds happiness in all our races
And swells the freedom song that we're a part.

We are the painters
That will sketch tomorrow.
We are the poets that will paint today.
We are the mourners
Born of all your sorrows.
We are the pavers that will pave the way.

Thank you God for bringing us together.
The rainbow that for all
These lives we've longed.
These are our open thoughts.
These are our open hearts.
This is our precious, precious freedom song.

The Everyman

Here rests the Everyman,
Most humble in his stance,
Who walked beneath the sun
Until he died.

Here rests the Everyman,
Calloused hands and feet,
Weather worn and wearied,
Until he died.

Here rests the Everyman,
Sweltered night and day,
Whose children thanked him not
Until he died.

Here lies the Everyman,
Beneath the worms and dirt,
Who hurt neither man nor child,
Until he died.

Here lies the Everyman
Who smells of putrid hell,
Whom man said lived so purely
Until he died.

Here lies the Everyman
Who saw the world as is,
And lived like every man
Until he died.

Here stands the Everyman
Engaged in mortal thought,
Who'll blindly walk the earth...
Until he dies.

Where Am I Today?

Where am I today
That I wasn't yesterday
And I won't be tomorrow?
Feeling a little bit
Under the weather
And a little bit frustrated
Because the world doesn't
Turn by my whim.
Once upon a time,
Years ago,
I had a dream
The rain was falling
And I was a star
Shinning through the dim
So bright that the
Sun came out to play
And dried up all the rain.
Sometimes,
I'm walking alone, cold
And afraid
And I see that star
And I run to that star
Breathless and sure.
But, stopped in my tracks,
I put down my things
And open my coat
And the stream that
Runs from me
Is a thousand dreams,

And the breath that
Runs from me
Is a thousand promises
I have broken to myself.

What will I be tomorrow
That I haven't become
Today?

From the Mind

Jumbled poetry, round and round,
Pregnant with the dark
More time lost.
Closed minds, infringed hate,
Family devotion betrayed.
Jilted seduction applied.
Drunk on thoughts,
A troubled man sleeps fine,
Sick with basement profanity,
Attentions met.
Enveloped in watery swelter
Floating, floating
Bobbin drowsily through time
Cascading pond frozen
Robin flying
Everyman dying
Blue skies fantasy
Down to earth
Slowly think
Spilling forth and frothing
From the mind.

Once upon a Time

When we were younger
Budding bright, once upon a time,
Wonder stories on our tongues
And friendship in our hearts,
Swallowed up in make-believe
Of ages, ages hence,
We played.
Now, time has gone
Deeds are done,
I can finally say
I miss being on
My knees, scampering
For joys.
Our world was colored paper,
Our imaginations, toys.
But oh, we've grown
And shed our youth.
I hate to love you now.
You broke the pact
And left the toys to dust.
For one brief moment,
In my life,
I've returned to find
That yes, you left behind
The vow
To love and grow and share
Once upon a time.

But I Won't Forget

I'll never forget
The day I knew
That Kansas was a dream,
Born to a world
Where the only
Protection I had
Was my silence
And the only
Salvation I had
Was my sin.
My stutter,
The long, dramatic
Decline into loneliness,
Twisted up in make-believe
Of some day…some day.
I remember the days
You banished me from
Your world
After bringing me into your life
And send me hurling into adulthood
Sick and afraid.
I never had a childhood,
And I always needed one.
I'll forgive, but won't forget
Because,
I refuse to forget the night
You bashed me like
A rusty nail
And I fell

Too hurt to fight.
I refuse to forget the nights
You slurred the words
I love you
Too many times
With too much guilt.
I became the
Bah, bah black sheep
And gave you all my wool,
Three pages full
And now,
I'm done.
I've left alone the lonely,
Fantasy driven nights
To come home to the
Good times of the past,
Because you understood
The Colour Green,
Unlocked the garden gates
And, in your own way,
Let me be the man
That I've become.
You loved my love
And set me free
And I became a son.

So, I'll remember
The wonder stories,
The laughter and the songs.
I'll draw from the strength
I have stored,
Knowing that all bad times

Will turn good
As they should.
For every bad memory
It takes ten bright ones
To make you forget.
Some day I may,
But, today,
I haven't yet.

Dear Daddy

Dear Daddy—
Why the hell have you forsaken me,
Your only worthwhile son?
Because I wear the Colour Green?
Because I wear your hidden shades?
You are the man that
Grinds me to the
Blood and bone.
But, dear Daddy,
You can't forget me.
My eyes are yours
Three-fold.
I have seen and heard
The things you may deny.
I'm so sorry I'm not holy
In your kingdom hall of hate.
No, I'm not!
There is no change,
So you can have your throne
Made of my bones.

Sing your sorry lullabies,
I won't await your trust.
I need you less
Than when I was a child.
Don't rock-a-bye me
With your sad,
Sweet tunes of unsung guilt.

I am a stronger man
That Noah built.

Yes, I am a real Man,
Daddy,
Despite what you may think.
I turned out better than fine.
I never had a daddy
And I never needed one.
Can you say the same
For all your other bastard sons?

Sinner, sinner,
Sinner hell,
Why don't you
Take a chance and tell—
How many boys
By how many different
Wives, harem daddy?
Take back
Your books of wisdom.
Read them well.
I didn't need them,
Or the verses
Thrown as weapons
From your pulpit, Daddy.

Tell me, Daddy,
Since we're sharing,
Are you cringing?
Are you swearing?
Suicide had nothing at all

To do with the loss of you.
With Mommy telling lies,
And Daddy feeling hate,
All that's left for me to do
Is stand and wait.

Who are you,
Dear, dear Daddy?
Is there a book
That I can read
That tells of all the
Sordid deeds,
That you laid at
Our God's feet
And then forgot?
Did you list your
Next of kin,
Did you
Write of all your sins
That you passed down
To the only worthwhile
Son that you begot?

One day,
I'll see my daddy
For the man that
He's become—
So frosted over with his
Guilt and loss.
How dare you judge me,
Daddy,
When you didn't see me walk,

You didn't hear me talk,
When you didn't see me grow
Into a man?
To re-invent myself
Required awful, damned good skill.
You didn't know me then,
So refuse to love me now
For, no one knows
The places I have been.

You don't know me,
You don't love me.
You can't change me,
So what of me?
I'll tell you what—
Sit back
And turn the page.

My Faith Can Swallow You

Let's all go down
To the temple of hypocrisy
And see what folks
Are wearing
Who is sharing
People swearing
As they walk all over you.
There ain't no shame in
What I do.
My faith can swallow you.

Let's take a ride
On the dragon-beast
And say it's
Innocent fun.
We'll tip the Jezebel
Flat on her back
And tomorrow morn,
Take it all back.
There ain't no shame in
What I do.
My faith can swallow you.

Then, on judgment day
Let's slip on our frocks
And dust off our shoes
And don our new smocks
Let's slide on our rings
And all fancy things

And swear that we take
It all back.
But, there ain't no shame in
What I do.
My faith can swallow you.

And the slaughtered lamb
Will take my hand
And you'll all wonder why
Because I didn't lie
In the temple of hypocrisy.
Just wait your turn
And when you all burn,
There's no absolution to buy
And my faith will swallow
You and you and you
And, oh, you too.

Boy in the Mirror

I got rid of you
A hundred years ago
With your mealy-mouth
And puppy dog eyes and
Vacant stare.
Fearful of the dark
And dogs that bark
But here you are again,
My friend
Staring at me from that mirror
As if I'd let you in—
You who sings in a whisper
But fears in a shout!
Get out!
Get out of here with your
Sadness and woe and
Cringing from sharp tongues.
It's the courage you lack
That invented me—
Tall, defiant and angry.
Angry at the fact that
The future us will
Hate me too
As I hate you
Little Boy Blue.
Living had nothing at all
To do with the likes of you
Pining for dear Daddy
And keeping

Pictures of pious people
Who don't even know
Who you really are.

Further from the Mind

Prince of depression
Tough guy,
Unerring touch of gold.
Seven days to glory.
Is justice not a word?
Cheap trick,
Slave of lust
Hot breeze on cold skin
Water soul will see you all in hell.
Xanax queen,
Crown of pills,
Bitch friend to the end.
Dead cat coming back
To claim his tail.
The Rhymer Man,
Siren screech,
Waterfall of thought.
Broken hearted.
More than I deserve.
Stomach vice,
Take a puff of
Gentle forms of hate.
Rainbow nation,
Frog and toad are friends.
Mind wander,
Wonder Boy,
Tilting on a brink.
Nothing more to drink.
Forcing me to think.

Falling fast
And
Further from the mind.

The Death of My Awakening

I am mourning
The death of my awakening
As the tick-tock of time
Launches all memories
Into staleness,
And the show is finally done.
I have sought the last curtain call,
Consumed the final toast
To the dearly departed
World I loved so well.
But where there is end
Begins anew another
World with a bright, new sun
And a dazzling moon
And voices that rise in sorrow
For the thousands of ages
Which have already passed.
I am mourning the beckoning
Of the wind-chime flute song
Echoing the dark passage
That turns friends to enemies
And, as that longing subsides,
I am mourning
The death of my awakening.
If I answer to
Silver-tongued existentialists
Drowning in their own desire
To be unreal,
Questioning the artistry of soul,

Then I become the hypocrite
That stalks the true meaning
Of every other gesture
When my own gestures
Only tend to lie.
I'd lose the reason why
And, I'd mourn myself for
All that I've become.
Instead, I remain the
Silent, cautious soul-mariner
Mourning the death of my awakening.

Dream

I wake to find you gone beside me.
I rise and wipe the sleep from my face,
Stretching in the sunlight.

I walk over to our window to look out over the day.
I see her, a girl in a doll's dress and doll's face.
"May I?" she asks as she glides in
Through the open window.
Others follow,
Each color richer than the last.
I ask, "Are you from costuming?"
"No," they answer, gathering around.
I see the costumer in the corner and I am surrounded,
Pretty maids all in a row, harlequins all,
Poised for a costume ball.
I'll have them yell "Surprise" when you enter,
I think to myself.
A morning party in our bedroom.
I move to answer the telephone,
But somehow, I know that you already have, elsewhere.
Somehow, I know it is your call.
Vividly, I replace the receiver,
Missing once, but finding the cradle the second time.
Foreshadowing.
I worry that you will take my clumsiness
For eavesdropping.
"Don't you want to come with us?" The doll asks me
As a menagerie joins us at the window.
Weakly, I answer, "No. I am in love."
And they are gone.

I leave the bedroom
To find you whispering
On the telephone. Why?
I lay beside you on the sofa
And gaze up to take in your beauty.
"Who are you speaking to?"
I ask you.
But you answer me angrily, not an answer at all,
"Do I question you?"
I am honest. "Yes."
"It is my business," you say
And suddenly, I know.
"Give me the marker so that I may wipe it out,"
You growl to me.
I move slowly,
As in a dream.
I retrieve the marker atop the television
And I deliver it to you.
You wipe away the truth.
Defeated, I walk toward the bedroom.

I am fully dressed.
You ask me where I am going.
It is the hardest decision I have ever made,
And I tell you.
We discuss my leaving,
But you show no remorse.
What has happened is clear to both,
But unmentionable.
I know. You know I know.

We turn and enter the restaurant.
There, I purchase my ticket from a machine.
It is an airplane ticket,
Though I have never flown.
You do not deny anything.
You do not ask me to stay.
You do not tell me you are sorry.
You do not tell me you love me.
"Where are you going?" You say instead.
"I don't know."
I answer. I don't know where I am.

She is sitting at a table in the distance.
We see her. You join her.
You feel nothing for me.
She smiles radiantly and waves.
I say good-bye.
"No!" She says. "Stay!" She says.
Sadly, I shake my head in denial.

Then, he appears, carrying a tray.
Hot, angry passion envelops me
As tears strain at the blockade of my lid.
I shiver, but refuse to weep.
"Don't go," She whispers in the distance.
"Stay, join us."
"No," I answer, my tears pushing wildly to be set free.
"You'll come back," She says.
You and he turn in unison to look at me.
I shake my head in violent denial
As the tears spill forth.
They pour in torrents from my soul.

I weep until the very root of my soul is running dry,
Blindness.
I feel your hand on me and, sobbing gently…

I wake to find you beside me.
I rise and wipe the tears from my face.

Is It Too Much to Ask?

It's three o'clock
In the morning
And I finally realize that
Momma didn't name me
Jesus Christ
And I cannot solve the problems
Of the world.
How can I be anyone's savior
When I cannot save myself?
Our Father, of the mysterious ways,
Has granted me the power to heal.
Is it too much to ask
For the power to heal myself?

I cannot sing the song
You want to hear
While I'm chain smoking
In reflection.
How about a toast to
The undeniable power
To fail?
If I can give so much
Of myself
To everyone else,
Is it too much to ask
For some of myself in return?

I vow,
As many times before,

No more tender touches for you,
No more building of pyramids,
No more refilling of the soul,
No more late, dark nights of pity,
No more serenity,
No more waiting for
The boys that do,
No more pining for
The boys that don't.
Because I have
Lived so much life,
Is it too much to ask
For dreams that won't fade
Or burn?

I still want to go
Over the rainbow
To make my final wish.
I'm sick of being
Sick of being alone.
I want the songs I sing
Of the love I want
To have refrain.
Is it too much to ask for
Happily ever after
Without sorrow
Without bitterness
Without regret?
Is it too much to ask
That I forget
The stale rancor of reality,
Escape from the state

Of the world as I know it,
Cold and jaded,
Hungry for all the wrong things,
Controlled by the sun
Drying all the rain
And up and down the spout again?
All I have the courage to ask is—

Is it too much to ask?

Lady

Lady walks into the
Bar at midnight
To camp out in dim light.
Insomnia beckons,
The migraine threatens,
As she orders her first drink.
Se looks up at the bartender
And tells him,
"I can feel the rain
At the bottom of my heart."
Can I have another?
Melancholy,
She loves this song.
Nostalgia.
Lost
And virginally insane
She's running…
And running…and running,
Changing faces,
Changing names
But always hoping
That one day
She'll be safe from herself.
Lost.
She needs nurturing
And finds it
In whisky and coke
And glamour sticks
And hunted men

A thousand.
Lady's in bad humor.
"Men suck, but women
Are psychotic."
She looks into the cracked mirror
And hates the shape of
Her face and the wave of her hair
And the curve of her lips
But she knows that men
Love her.
But she knows that she
Hates men.
Sometimes,
Death is a lighthouse
Beckoning its ship safely
Home
Way back to 'Bama.
With a cigarette
In one hand and
A suitcase in the other,
Lady's searching for
Prince Charming
But the prince has got no name.
And so, she waits.
She's trying on glass slippers
But can't seem
To make the match,
The man huntress with
Broken arrow and bow.
As her song plays on
The jukebox,
Her desire fills the glass

"Down the hatch."
Lady, oh Lady,
Dear Lady,
Are you blind
To all the beauty
All the splendor
All the pain?
Take this hand I
Leave outstretched.
I'll take your shame
You take my strength
And together we'll
Make the demons
Flying mad.
But she turns from
Her reflection,
A muse without direction
Takes a sip—
A cigarette
And strikes a match.
Cloudy girl of woe,
A mistress of despair,
You'll call her
Lady luck.
I'll call her, Brandy dear.

Thoughts on a Summer Day in July

Disquieted
Unsettled and unsatisfied
Tilting on the edge of depression
Balancing on the brink of life.
I want so much
Have so little
Reaching out to turn on a light
That will wipe away the
Darkness.
I am a child who lies in
The night, fearing that there's
Something coming to get me
And hearing the noises that
Remind me I'm missing
Something somewhere else.
I am homesick
But I have no idea
Where home is.
Cut off form the rest of the world
By independence
Wanting so much to be nothing
But needing so much to be everything,
One extreme to another.
Teased because I was hopeless
And now glorified because I am hopeful
But I feel no glory in myself and I
Wonder at that faith which
Draws others to me.
Why does everyone love him

Who hates himself so?
I don't understand this need to
Live without questions.
Thinking will be my downfall.
Once the mind grasps reality
The explosion is all encompassing
From the inside out and
From the mind.
The dance is one of
Razor blades and gas filled rooms
A pill for every thought.
It is not enough to be
Quiet, settled and satisfied
Because once we lose the
Power to reach we have lost
The magic of dreams.
Yet, having such power
I sit awake and daydream
Rather than abandoning
False security and making dreams real.
So I sip my coffee of the day
And read the dreams that
Other men have written
While mine go unlived.
I don't care that I drink too much
Smoke too much.
I care to love from
A distance because that
Is the only thing that's
Safe for my heart.
Where it is dark
Somewhere else it is light

And someone is ambitious enough
To dance naked
While I am ambitious enough
To talk about how I want
To dance naked.
The flies enjoy my lunch
While I starve out the stories
Of my life
And as the man passes by
He wonders why the hell
I sit here all alone
Sipping java that
Was long ago cold
When there's so much
To see and do on this
Bright summer day
In July.
He doesn't understand
That it is sometimes
Enough to sit and think
About why nothing is
Being done.
I sometimes need to nourish
The Sylvia Plath inside me
So she won't get too disquieted
And take over—dance me
Into a corner and turn on
The flame without a flame.
When I think that I want
To die as much as I want
To live, then the two cancel
One another like an equation

And I end up doing neither.
I don't want to be just another
Cover song done until I am stale
But the melodies that make up
My life repeat themselves forever.
My life sentences become unpunctuated
And no one gives me more than a glance.
So here's to God and all the angels
Who look down at me and whisper and
Giggle because I
Have become such an Everyman.
And whatever may or may not be,
Every man I am not.

Part Two

Some Boys Do

Fingerprints

Love comes differently
Each time it comes,
Sometimes it takes a minute
Sometimes a day
Sometimes a lifetime,
But each time it does,
It marks the heart
With tiny fingerprints
That never wash away.

Thank You for Breaking My Heart

You keep me tragic,
But they won't see me cry
And shatter all the images
I've made.
Momma knows no truth
And Daddy knows no shame
But brother knows them all
And you're to blame.
Thank you for breaking my heart.

You're the d nouement of happiness,
The waking from a dream,
The crash of a buzz,
Monday.
And the teacher knows no answers.
The preacher knows no god.
You are the total eclipse
Of my bright day.
Thank you for breaking my heart.

I Didn't See

I didn't mean to stare at you
As you picked away for food.
And when you pushed your
Plate away,
I didn't see you move.

I didn't mean to watch you
As you wiped your
Sweaty brow.
I didn't see you turn to look,
'Cause I'm not watching now.

I didn't see you stroke your chin
Nor lick your thick, red lips.
I didn't see you rub your chest
And shake the crumbs from it.

I didn't see you strike that match,
I didn't watch it burn.
I didn't see you notice
As I turned away and squirmed.

I didn't see you watch me
As I walked away at last.
But I could feel you staring
As you stroked your empty glass.

One Night

Come in,
Sit down,
Unwind, unlock, embrace,
Step out of light.
It's a dark and scary place
Because it's our first time tonight.
I haven't been here often.
I transform and
Out again
To climb the walls
And search the night
For one true, special friend.
Come and get to know me.
After dark, I'm so much fun.
At the end of this encounter,
I'll know you're not the one.
But, for now, I'll just enjoy
Such sweet scents and candlelight.
After all, a one night stand
Won't even last the night.

Sleazy

You say you hate the thought
Of my sweet male body
Pressing against your own,
And yet you move closer and closer
Into the realm of destruction—
A bully running from
Your own Green shadow,
Fawning over the possibility
That dreams may come to light.
Lounge lizard
With a quick smile
And a serpent walk,
Sleazy man,
You are not as deceptive
As you seem
Or would like to be.
I see through you like a
Pure shard of glass
Broken in my step.
And I see your pain.
I feel your glare
As I walk across the room.
Cable knit in guilt
For your own affection.
And I am constantly attracted
To the gruff, sleazy
Way of your world.
I purr when you bark at me,
While your bashfulness

Reaches deep
Into my cold, dark soul
That clutches at
Dank, devious, dissention
From my norm.
Like I do for those who
Break my heart,
I cling to your destruction
Of me.
If I repeat my history
I'll need you when
You least need me,
Sleazy.

Sigh

If I could ever make
Time stand still,
I'd be in your arms,
Lost in your charms
Fresh and unbroken,
Fornication and carnal knowledge.
Come, darling,
Undress.
Lie down.
Let me get your ready.
Can I taste your virginity
Until it dries
Hot on my lips,
Moist on my thighs?
Erupt your volcano
As I
Lie you down,
Make love to you
Flesh to flesh,
Body to body,
Blood to blood,
Mano a mano,
Ashes to ashes,
Dust to dust,
Sweat to sweat,
And musk to musk.
If I hurt you,
Lover, don't fret.
Take a deep breath.

Don't ask to stop.
Pause,
Whimper,
Shake,
Glimmer
And
Sigh.

Guilt

Tick-tock goes the tell tale heart
As you think about the thing
You've done and with whom.
You fidget as you see
Knowledge in the eyes of
Everyone you meet.
Ever titter, snort, snick
Becomes a personal demon
As your neat, little world
Comes undone,
Unraveled, crumpled
At your feet,
Shuffled up in shame, regret;
Head pounding
Wishing you could
Pause, rewind, and re-think,
Take the early train,
Refuse that final drink.
No such magic saves you
As you pass like a phantom—
Head down
Walk of shame,
A man in self-inflicted
Purgatory for a curiosity
Too strong to resist.
You pass me,
But deny the urge
To speak,
As I turn my head

And sip my drink
And fan myself
Too leisurely.

Jimmie

He swaggers up to me
Like a tall, lean, virgin
Drink of piña colada.
He is actually
More intoxicating than even
The strongest liquor,
And more relaxing than any herb.
Jimmie—
With his hair like
A dense jungle at midnight;
His smile blinding me
Like a solar eclipse,
Wrapping me in a toasted blanket
Of security and wisdom.
His laugh is like a magic carpet
That sweeps me up
Into the stars and
Tips me over to fall
Down, down, down
Back into the coffee eyes
That know truth and
Dance in dim light.
Southern comfort in
Golden skin as perfect
As a newly swept
Caribbean beach by moonlight;
A voice that leaps
And wraps tightly around words,
Bathing them in

A sweetness that falls upon,
And graces the ears.
A gentleman of all ages.
Strong enough to deny my charms,
And yet gentle enough
To allow just a bit of flattery.
Just a bit.
Quiet, with a presence
Like a Native deity
And the calming power
Of a gentle rain
In springtime.
He swaggers up to me,
A tall, lean drink of
Southern comfort—
I sigh deeply,
Regretfully almost.
And I smile.

Dormant

Love is like a mountain
So majestic, bold and pure
And sometimes a volcano,
Powerful, deadly and sure.

Mine for you was dormant,
But now wants to erupt,
And I follow you so silently,
As the first time this fire lit up.

So when you brushed against me,
My soul was set aflame.
So fervent was my passion
That lust drove me insane.

Breathless, I adored you.
With quickened pulse, I stared.
But when you lingered near me,
To move, I seldom dared.

Your flesh was molten lava.
In pools of sweat we burned.
The dark was a welcome whisper,
As desire within me churned.

But you put aside my burning,
And I now stand alone,
While I wait again to receive you
Like a trembling cinder cone.

Imagine

Imagine for a moment
That you love me.
What do you love?
My strength, devotion,
My sadness, my temperament,
My movement like the rushing wind?
Imagine for a moment
You hunt me.
Where?
On the golden isle,
By sea, jungle,
Air?
And then
You mount me
And I love you.
Your star-shine,
Blueness, depth.
And I carry you
As you carry me
Licking tongues of flame.
What then?
Your sun melts into my sea,
Washing flood of fire,
Emotion,
As when you look at me.
Imagine I bow my head and cry
Because you are only imagining.
Are you?

I Die

Can you possibly know of
All the tears I store inside?
I am desperate to destroy
The blazing pain I cannot hide.
You see the strength,
The chiseled stance,
I harbor only wounded pride.
For each time I gaze upon you,
I die.

Do you care, is it a farce,
The world just touch and go?
The suicidal dare?
To finally let you know
That you decipher childish fancy
From a pain too strong to abide,
For every time you speak to me
I die.

I die when I'm beside you
I die when I'm alone.
I die when I am loving you,
But no one really knows.
My life is on a stage.
My emotions are a show
In which I cry and cry and cry and cry…and cry.
Hoping that the pain will end,
I die.

Stage Kiss

The light burns hot on my neck.
Your sweat trickles down, down
To melt into me.
Your body heat sweeps over me.
My stomach flutters.
The audience titters on
The edge of its seats,
Inhale as one.
I inhale your deep, sensual odor.
I forget the watchers.
You part your lips in slow motion.
I can smell the sweet moistness.
My mouth waters, my body aches
My ears buzz
As your hair brushes my face.
You pull me closer,
Man to man.
Your lips tickle mine,
First bottom, then top.
Our eyes close.
The audience breathes
Deeper still.
I melt.
The curtain falls.

Trek

I want to be swept away
In the depth of your eyes,
Whirl through space,
Alight on the soft, sandy
Beaches of your skin,
Soak in the glow
Of your smile and be washed on the shore
By the waves of your kisses
To safari in the jungle of your hair,
Swinging through the
Twisting vines
To hike through the mountains
Of your muscular frame
And pitch tent close to your heart,
Rise early in your sunlit smile
To find my true destiny—
Home
In the temple of your body.

He Loves Me Not

He loves me, he loves me not—
Which, I do not know.
He is everything and everyone,
The dark knight, the white knight,
The truth, the light, the dark, falsehood, love.
He loves me, loves me not.
I lie to myself
One way or another,
Depending upon the circumstances—
Playing blind, playing wise.
He loves me, loves me not.
Regardless of what they say,
It's what he thinks,
What I feel,
'Though I do not know.
He loves me, loves me not.
He tells me, I can't believe.
It's not the love I want or need
But the only love he can give,
The only love allowed—
The friendship that breaks my arrow
With stolen glances, kisses, and words of
He loves me, he loves me not.
In my eyes, he does no wrong.
In my eyes, he does no right.
I'm hurt, and yet, I heal
And return to reburn the wounds
That give the certain answer—
He loves me, loves me not.

Daddy Longlegs

Daddy Daddy Longlegs
You appear before me
Stranger than my father
With visions of sugar plums
Dancing on my bed.

Daddy Daddy Longlegs
Your punk rock
Rocks my mind
Lo and behold
You walk away
But your face has stained my brain.

Daddy Daddy Longlegs
Bottle me up
Set me off shore
Nibble with your fish tongue
And fins slapping against the cork
Set me free.

Oh, Daddy Daddy Longlegs
Come breath life into me
Your goatee tickling my vein
Caress me with long nails
Scratch the surface
Dig below.

Daddy Daddy Longlegs
Red leather and cocaine breath

Candles burning
Binding spells
From one to nine.

My heart belongs to
Daddy Daddy Longlegs
Tea with cream and sugar
Crumpets and English muffins
And a smile.

Daddy Daddy Longlegs
With your hands that
Stick like glue
Come to me and let me show you
Just what I can do.

Daddy Daddy Longlegs
Swift and smooth as fire
Hot desire, melting
Crisping, breaking
Burn me.

The Chambers of My Mind

Venture forth into the chambers of my mind
Where deep voices groan the unhappiness of time
And we are climbing a stinging vine from the
Dark, carelessness of nothing into
The bright freshness of everything.
You and I
Yen, yang
Tomorrow night at day
Moon set fantasy
Unwinding on a velvet road into
The chambers of my mind.
I yearn to call you by your
One true given name
—Lover.
To see you alone is a blessing
To have you alone is a dare.
How I long to understand and embrace
The stillness and the silence
Of your sweet dare.
Is there anyone in creation
Who longs to know as much as I?
There is a lightning storm whipping around
In your soul
As I dream to draw you into my abyss
Chain you up with my sweetness
Tie you down with care
Harbor your eccentricities in
The chambers of my mind.
Molasses tongued

Night child,
Moon Goddess born,
Would wed your depression and
Take it to her heart.
But sexual tendency flows
And draws you away from that point,
A point so mute that even
I only ponder it in
The chambers of my mind.

What I Can Do

Come to me and
Let me show you
Just what I can do.

I can eat your heart
Like liver
And spit it out un-chewed.
I can make you
Want my sword
To pierce your
Bloody heart right through.
I can make you curse
The testament, your mother, father—
There's no use resisting
All the pain that
Cracks your brain—
And then
I'll glue you up with excrement
And thrash you 'til
Your brown eye turns to blue.
Come to me and
Let me show you
Just what I can do.

I can hypnotize and paralyze
Burn you with a match.
Run to me, don't walk to me
Sit down and take the
Hatchet buried deep inside

The dripping eyes—
Pain
Through, through and through.
Come to me and
Let me show you
Just what I can do.

I can tie you up
And lie you down
And whip you like a whore.
Don't talk to me
Just watch and see
The blood run from your—
There's no use resisting all
The pain that cracks your brain
And tortures you.

Come, sweetheart, and
Let me show you
Just what I can do.

Taste

I want to taste the salty
Peak of desire,
Inhale the sweet, musky
Smell of man,
Tickle my skin on your fur and
Taste the full smoothness
That makes us whole—
Lather and lace you with kisses
Tire my tongue and buzz my lips
Celebrate texture, pleasure,
Pain, sensation—
Hear nothing but the
Sound of your heartbeat as
The blood pulses
Through your thighs—
Taste your heartbeat against
My teeth and tongue
And rock you until you
Shudder from grief and pain,
Triumph and pleasure
All at once
And fall from grace
To breathlessly adore me.

You Told Me I'm the One

Gleaming eyes that filch my pride
And leave me mortified
For what I've done.

I gave you all of me.
You gave me less that truth.
And all the while,
You told me I'm the one.

You jabbed your hands
And gashed my chest,
Ripped away my heart.

I gave you all of me.
You gave me less that truth.
And all the while,
You told me I'm the one.

I trusted you
To keep me from
This pussing, wounded carcass
I've become.

I gave you all of me.
You gave me less that truth.
And all the while,
You told me I'm the one.

I crave your death.
Spew on your grave.
My shame has come undone.

I gave you all of me.
You gave me less that truth.
And all the while,
You told me I'm the one.

I'll dance 'til dawn
And defecate your memory
'Til it's gone.

I gave you all of me.
You gave me less that truth.
And all the while,
You told me I'm the one.

You lied to me.
You cheated me
And left when you were done.

I gave you all of me.
You gave me less that truth.
And all the while,
You told me I'm the one.

You bastard.

Blue-Collar Man

Blue-collar man
With a blue collar tan
And blue collar body
With a blue collar gate
And blue collar morals—
Be my blue-collar mate.

Nothing can take the place
Of my blue-collar man.
He smells of
Cigarettes and beer and sweat
And occasionally sex.

I take him
In my hands,
Body so lean and strong,
And massage away
The stress.

I feed him like a child
And coo and pet
And tease.

I relax him in the
Hottest water
Man has ever known,
Strip away the grit and grime
And make him feel at home.

When he rises
From the filth of the day,
Tall and rugged and tan
He comes to me
So bronze and free
And I'm proud to be a man.

Nothing can take the place
Of my blue-collar man.
Nothing.

Darling Martyr

Did you tell her
You love her
Before she left
That day
On a nonexistent journey
To a nonexistent place
For a nonexistent meeting
With her nonexistent kin
Into the waiting arms
Of your underhanded friend
To turn over and over and over
In your blindness
As you slept away the day
In your trustful stupor,
Darling Martyr?
Did she tell you
As she threw you
To the wolves
Of a world so cruel
To those who have been hurt,
Darling Martyr?
Are you
Once bitten, twice shy
Too much of a man to admit
That you're such a man
To cry
And lie about the sneaky
Way she broke
Your heart, your trust, your home

—Left you and the child alone,
Darling Martyr?
Did you tell you
That you love yourself
When you finally said good-bye
Did you lie,
Or did you really think it so,
Darling Martyr?
Did you wait for her
To call you
When she climbed
Out from her artificial,
Faithless, broken love?
Now, do you move a little
Closer out of fear
I'll also go
On a nonexistent journey
To a nonexistent place
For a nonexistent meeting
With a nonexistent friend
For a underhanded tryst
That will bring our love to end,
Darling Martyr?
You don't yet have to worry.
My desire hath no hurry.
I'll stay with you
'Til morning,
Darling Martyr.
And 'til dawn,
I'll dry your tears
And the sun will dry your fears
In the morning when we wake,
Darling Martyr.

Too Selfish to Be Lonely

It's four in the morning and I'm wondering
Where you are,
Who you're with and holding close
And if you're thinking of me.
Impossible
To believe that you were drawn to me
Of your own free will.
I'll think what I will,
That I'm a pawn
In a sick, cosmic game of chess,
Too selfish to be lonely
Too lonely to set you free.
You take me to places I've never been
And give me reason to believe
That life is not a song played over again
But a new song I can sing.
I'm too selfish to be lonely
And too lonely to set you free.
I'm too afraid of the light that shines
Through my window
When the morning has come too soon and
Too afraid of the moment we part
When we both have things to do.
I feel too selfish to be lonely.
I feel too selfish to set you free.
And, in a million years
You'll never really love me.
Please, don't be too selfish to be lonely
And don't be too lonely to set me free.

Golden Boy

I'm giving you
Back to her
As if you were
A jewel
Laid at my feet
Who pined the
Warm embrace
Of something strangely gentle.
You shy away from
The awful truth that
You could love one
Who left a trace
Of the man hungry
For the life long feast.
She is the only true jewel
That you enjoy
Young, worthwhile boy.
I want you to be safe.
Contradict the true embrace
And hide from me.
What makes you so insane,
My golden boy,
Everyman I want
But can never truly have?
The heart and the flesh
Are enemies
To the end,
My golden boy.
Rusty colored nail

Me to my own
True sense
Of responsibility
And moral justice to leave you alone.
Run from me,
The wind in our hair
As I watch you
Make a turn into the Heather
Back to your
Familiar, lonely
Puckish life.
No furrow to the brow, dear boy.
What exactly are you
Hiding from me,
Golden boy?
You start, then stop
The tale,
Reflect, exhale.
The true, ironic tale
Is that
You followed me
Before I followed you
And, when you awake
From your deep sleep,
You'll realize
That some boys do.
Please, don't genuflect
To me, Golden Boy.
You are the one,
True prodigal son
Of royal love,
As golden as your nectar

And as innocent as a
Born free dove
Racing from society.
Though your years
Are more than mine,
I am a serious man
Far beyond your grasp.
Your rosy focals
Paint my world
In glamour,
Admired by your fantasy.
But my fantasy of you
Is as golden
As a blazing
Summer sun.
How do we end this
Cruel ploy of truth?
Tell me.
Let me know,
Will you approach me
As a man
Or as a frightened
Golden boy?

My Funny Boy

Hello, Yankee boy.
What a beautiful night,
What a beautiful man,
What a wonderful soul.
I look at you and I see happiness.
I talk to you and I feel your pain,
All alone, so far away, over the rainbow.
My funny boy.
My Greek Marine.
My Everyman that's clean.
You are my own personal
Greek tragedy
And we can live and die
Together as we battle
Our invisible foes
On the shores of
Themyscira.
Let me hold you in the coldness.
I sing the songs of old.
You will be okay, someday,
But today, you cry into my pillow
And I rock us to deep sleep,
So deep.
Please remember,
My funny boy,
My Greek Marine,
My every boy that's clean
I love you for your
Fantasyland of lovers

As beautiful as you.
I wish you knew.
You're the kind of man
I fall for,
The kind that breaks my heart.
Lay down your weapons
And come to me.
Dance the sexy Greek dances
That lay me down to sleep
On a beautiful night
With a beautiful man
With a wonderful soul
My funny boy
My Greek Marine
My every soul that's clean.

Forever

How I wish I could
Go back in time,
When you were here
Not for a day,
But forever.

But yesterday
Seems far away.
When you're not here,
Then everyday is
Forever.

Once upon a time,
In a land not far from here,
I met a love who held me.
Whispered in my ear
As he held me near
Love is crystal clear
Forever.

Happily ever after,
Running free and wild.
But he had to leave me,
Not forever,
For a while.

As I turn the pages,
As the story roams,
I can't find the chapter

Where the prince
Comes home.

Darling click your heels,
Carriage turn your wheels,
Children fill the hills with song.
I'll lay down my head,
Sleepy, sleepy head
And I'll dream
It won't be long.

But how long is a lifetime,
Is it only as long as a dream?
And is my heart breaking?
And is my soul aching?
Is it once upon a time?
Was it only for a time?
For I'll love you for all time....
Forever.

Nature's Love

I imagine love in springtime,
A surging ocean tide.
I imagine me a seashell
With all the sea inside.

I envision you a gentle breeze
That sweeps across my skin
And leaves the moisture of the rain
With the pressure from the wind.

You're the storm that blows against me
Upsetting what is new,
With a force and gale of strangeness,
But the warmth and feel of you.

I imagine then an earthquake,
A trembling from the base
That upsets the heart, but calms the soul
When nature's love takes place.

Whisper

I stumbled upon a twilight zone
In which time went still
And back again.
You planted in me
The turbulence of the cosmos.
Your love fills me with the
Mysticism of the universe.
If I could paint a portrait
Of our love, the colors would not be
Bright enough, the canvas wide enough.
Trust you?
How could I resist?
You rise from monotony,
A fleshy angel,
No order, no restraint,
Sweet skin enflaming my tongue.
God of discretion, cover me
As I delve into hot pools of lust.
We communicate wordlessly,
Idle rich with probing desire.
The poetic passion of love
Sweeps down like the phoenix
To rescue us from
Ashes to ashes, dust to dust
And as you stand bare on the shore.
I am the water that laps at your feet.
I am the moonlight that kisses your shoulders.
I am the tear that caresses your face.
When someone asks what true love is,

I gesture to you.
If someone asks, "What is devotion?"
Gently,
I whisper your name.
I whisper and I know that you hear me,
Through the cosmos,
The colors,
The phoenix
The night
The passion
The fire
Through love.

Heaven

This is our Heaven,
The night
And the stars
You...and I.
Kissing, holding, loving embrace
Dancing naked in the moonlight
Wine on our lips
Fire in our hearts
Flaming passions delight
And the height of ecstasy
As we reach into our souls
To find the world.
This is my Heaven,
In your eyes
In your body
In your tender, passionate kiss.
This is your Heaven,
In my trust
In my devotion
In my sleepless abandon.
This is our Heaven,
In love.

Complete

Sunlight,
Stretching softly
Over my skin
(my Body).
Mind frozen with
Delight at the touch,
The warming of the
Cold
(my Mind).
Stepping in from
The rain,
Stroking off wet
Drops of loneliness
Into an umbrella
Shielding me
(my Heart).
And the pounding
Of my heart
Becomes one with
Another,
A storm
(my Soul).
Blowing fiercely.
Twisting wildly.
Shouting frantically
(my Desire).
And then
Nature gathers me in
A bundle

(my Love)
To bathe me in
A sea of warmth
A rush of wind
A fire
Complete
In you.

Our Love

Our love is the dawn,
Appearing new each day,
Sprinkling soft dew,
Growing brighter and fuller.

It is the night,
Full, embracing,
Falling upon us as a blanket,
Softly whispering love poems.

It is a hot summer's day,
That beats like a drum
Strong and draining,
Subsiding,
Becoming, once again,
The night that melts into dawn.

Sing of My Sorrow

Precious angel
Come thou close.
Sing of my sorrow.

Doth he love me
As he boasts?
(Sing of my sorrow).

Then must my heart
Be torn asunder?
(Sing of my sorrow).

Must I rage
The tears of thunder?
(Sing of my sorrow).

He praises me not
Whilst he loves another
Killing so softly
I shan't recover.
Why am I slave
To an inconstant lover?
(Sing of my sorrow).

Must I now,
Until I die,
(Sing of my sorrow).

Devote my love
And fear his lies.
(Sing of my sorrow).

And if I should,
Could God forgive
That I lie down to die
Whilst he bids me to live
And avouch that I've given
All I can give.
(Sing of my sorrow).

I hear voices
Calling me.
(Sing of my sorrow).

Telling me truths
I'm blind to see.
(Sing of my sorrow).

The voices are mine
Dwelling deep in my brain.
They tell me I love him,
So I must be insane.
And, whilst I am dying
They doth not complain,
And yet
Sing, sing, sing,
Songs of my sorrow.

That's All I Need to Know

In fire, you kiss me,
I'm blinded by the flame.
You warm me and whisper that you care.
But you haven't told me
The reason that you cry.
You're hurting,
That's all I need to know.

I wake to find you,
The starlight calls your name.
I'm dreaming, yet I no longer sleep
But tears fall and drown you,
I reach…you turn away.
You're hurting,
That's all I need to know.

And it seems I'll never understand,
Understand anything that you do.
And 'though I've told you
I'll never hurt you
If I have
That's all I need to know.

You told me you wanted
A life I can provide
I kissed you and held you by the flame.
There's no need to tell me
The reason that you cry.
I love you.
That's all you need to know.

Us.

I set adrift on slumber's bliss
And from gray drowsiness
Color escapes the rainbow,
And I know love.
Us.
You take me in your arms
And dance me down a golden road
Up…up…up
Beyond the moon, beyond the rain,
The first kiss of the world
I become you become me become us become we
Become love.
I pause…
And totally exhale
As you reach deep inside of me to pick the fruit of my soul,
Wrapping me
In flaxen ecstasy
Silken wonderment
And velvet excitement
As we are
Shipwrecked on our island.
Us. Bliss.
Storm clouds billow
And you put down the umbrella.
Gray returns to blind me
Forty days and forty nights.
Finally, hand in hand we step into the light,
Shake ourselves dry, bittersweet but
Still Us…until the next time.

We laugh, we cry, we sing, we die
We resurrect and descend.
But the storm clouds hover.
We wed in starlight, star shine
Castles on clouds,
Knights in shinning armor
And Princes in distress,
Rescuing one another
With happy endings and ever afters.
But the pages turn and the book closes.
I knock my heels
And whirl around
The deck showers upon me
Us departs
And I wake to truth.
To grayness,
Wipe the sleep from my eyes
And rise.

Dark Knight

The dark dichotomy of your soul
Awakens me to
Curiosity and fear,
Wounded warrior in a
Strange new world,
Uprooted from your pain
And tossed and turned on a sea of anxiety.
Shipwrecked on the
Deserted island of
Regret and loss and shame,
Unable to sleep
For fear of dreaming,
Unable to wake
For fear of living alone,
You make friends into foes
And foes your comfort zone
In this new life of loneliness.
And, as I study your despair
From this weary affair,
All I can wonder is
How to breach the pain
And reach into the man-child's soul
So unable to feast of Eden.
Running from heart-break,
You're strapped to the rebel stallion,
Your hands clutching the reins,
Tear stained face buried in its mane,
Swept up in winds of anguish
On this,

Your self-created deserted island
Of shame.
And, as you fall
From your stead,
My dark, bruised hero,
To graze the dry, cracked
Earth of reality
And skid in a pool of tears,
How can I persuade you
To rise out of the gloom,
Dust the debris from your armor
And shine yourself anew?
What will it take to make
You ride again?
Once upon a time,
I thought that I
Could take control
Of every wayward
Soldier's soul,
But then, you came along
With your own private war
And I read your fortune
Out through me.
I make my final plea...
Come in from the
Tear polluted rain,
My silent, dark, torn knight
And rest a while with me
To see what the unsung break
Of tomorrow brings.

And You Don't Even Know

I told you the secrets
That I had stored inside.
You held me, and told me to cry.
But I haven't told you
The reason that I cry.
I love you,
And you don't even know.

You told me you wanted
A life I can't provide.
I held you, and told you, don't cry.
But I haven't told you
The reason that I cry.
I love you,
And you don't even know.

And the world will never understand,
Understand anything,
Like you do.
And 'though I've told you
I'll always trust you
I love you,
And you don't even know.

The rain falls around me
And I call out your name.
You answer, and that shows me you care.
But still I can't tell you
The secret of my life.
I love you and you don't feel the same.

And I haven't told you
The reason that I cry.
I love you,
And you don't even know.

All of You

Give me all of you
To chase away the pain of being alone.
Give me all of you.
Without it, we can't go on.
I know what I ask for is tough
But what I ask for, I pay for with love.
I need all of you,
Because part of you isn't enough.

I don't ask for the moon, the earth,
And I don't need the stars—
Empty promises thought to be love.
I need secure love—
A diamond in the rough,
A prayer…answered
When I call.

I need all of you.
I can't share the pain, so why share the love?
I need all of you.
Give up the unchaste desires I know of.
I keep having fantasies
Of a world where we soar like doves
And to find it,
I need all of you
And all of your love.

Go Away

Go away.
I don't need you now.
My pain is liquid fear
That I'll program
Into this truthful folly.
Go away from me
And liberate yourself
From my grasp.
Intoxicate my mind no more.
Give freedom to my heart.
Go away.
In time you will be pardoned
Of the grief that chains me down.
Move swiftly, and yet silently.
Free us without a sound.
Go away, go away, go away.

Stranger

Once again,
I've lost you,
Stranger with a simple name,
Golden boy with so much
Shame,
Who told me of wonderful,
Bright and beautiful things;
Who sat too close
But didn't care
And knew the depth of shade
And engaged me in the long
Sweet talk of manhood.
But, my artificial popularity
Came to haunt me
Once again.
I'm bitter at the
Falsehood that stole you
From my side—
Replaced by a cad,
Base, unforgiving and calloused.
Though I am surrounded,
I am alone.
Because you,
Beautiful, brave stranger,
Were gone but for a moment
But returned to find your
Nocturnal conquest conquered
And you left
Without a single trace,

Closing the open door behind you.
I pine what could have been,
At least for one fleeting hour
Like so many of my fleeting hours.

Little Man

Leave me alone,
Little man with
A big complex.
Napoleon was never
Such a cad,
As you trampled
An exotic flower
And left it to wilt.
But, the flower
Didn't wilt.
Sun, rain, snow, hail
Heartbreak
Cannot, will not
Damage the one, true
Reinvented stem.
You tiny, fleck of a man,
A true man understands
The need to grow and shine,
And independence is a medal.
But, you creep along
Medal-less
In this, the great
War of life
Without just a clue
Of greatness.

I Want to Be Me

Lightweight
Wants my body
To be his temple

Tantrum man
Wants my cool head
To be his heart

Christian man
Wants my soul
To be his savior

Drunk man
Wants my thirst
To be his own

I
Want me
To be me
Period.

Keeper of Souls

I am the keeper
Of men's souls.
When their dreams
Turn into rock salt
I am the
Satisfying dunk
Of redemption,
The halfway house
Of prodigal sons—
The one who can't
Say no.
My own dreams
Are all for naught.
I bottle them up,
Collect them,
And play with them
Like fireflies, caught.
I become the mirror.
They paint what they want
To see
In me
To be and never not to be
Completely for him.
Them.
Were my cupboards bare,
I would sail into
An anonymous sunset.
But my fireflies
Count on me

To nourish and protect them.
So I stay
For my cupboards are full
Of men's souls.

Magic Man

You arrived
Falling in from the clouds
Like a wizard
In a great balloon
From a far off
Land of make-believe
And fairy tales and songs—
The magic land,
Magic man.
That's exactly what you are—
A magic man that
Conjures tranquility and peace.

I could talk to you
For days without
Saying a single word—
Just looking into
Those eyes that comfort
For hours and hours
Until the jealous sun
Rises above damp buildings.
When you touched me,
It was as if
I hadn't been touched
Since birth.
My jailed soul was
Once again reborn.

I can close my eyes
And imagine
That lush garden
Built for two—
Waves crash on rocks—
A private boat
Tied up to a dock—
And how we laughed.
If I were to weep
I'd mourn
What never was
And never meant to be
But that's no longer me,
Magic Man.

When we bade farewell
And you climbed into
Your great balloon,
Sailed toward the stars,
I turned away
And suddenly,
I knew.
My Magic Man had
Turned a trick
In this side show
Called my life,
And the dreaded
Disappearing act
Has left no joy
To the Rhymer Boy.
You conjured something
Deep in my soul

That I thought
Had long ago died—
To grow as a seed
Under the tender
Care of the sun,
Rising, twisting and curling.
I felt something
Deep, strong and terrible
Missing for so long
—Just a touch of heartache.

I hummed a Magic Man
Love song.

Missing You

Every night the clock ticks in the hall.
The writing's on the wall.
I'm missing you,
And I want to see you again.
Every night I toss and turn away
The memories of the day.
I'm missing you,
And I want to be in your arms again.

Tonight, we said good-bye for the very last time.
Momma never told me that true love was a crime.
Our time together, I thought would last for always,
'Til the end of time—but time just slipped away.

In the days gone by, we became a little more than just friends
And made a journey to this moment when it all just ends.
We came together without sorrow, regret, without shame
To share a love—that dares not speak its name.

Time, stand still and let me enjoy
The kiss and tell
The pain and the joy.
If you stand still, I'm sure you will find
I'll deny my name,
Just say you'll be mine.

Two hearts entwined as we are
Could only live as a wish upon a star.
Tonight, we said good-bye for the very last time.

But, say that you'll remember me,
And I'll be fine.

Every night the clock ticks in the hall.
The writing's on the wall.
I'm missing you,
And I want to see you again.
Every night I toss and turn away
The memories of the day.
I'm missing you,
And I want to be in your arms again.

Some Boys Do

I'll climb onto the
Scaffold and stand
Awhile with you—
Share in your personal sin
And your shame.
The letter stings me
Just the same.

If I fall,
Will you catch me?
I will catch you
If you fall.

You wanted me
Before I wanted you.
Some boys do.
In my life,
You are not the first.
My biggest fear
Is that you will not
Be my last.

It started with
An old school chum,
A grain of pure respect—
Innocent love-lust,
Stumbling into the
Lost garden of delight,
Exiled in the closet
Of our own trust.

We,
Rolling around in
The underworld of
Lust and desire
Found that
In every truth there's folly
And in every folly there's truth.
Forbidden passion
Impacts the soul
And unlocks the
Man-fire to quench
A quiet urge.

Tell absolutely no one.
Of course,
I wouldn't dare.

And you,
You over there.

You sat and discussed
With me the conquests of
Your life with that
Hungry eye that only a
Man with a secret can have.
Your voice dripped like
Syrup spilling from the
Breakfast table while
Your smile gleamed like
A razor blade ready
To slice.
What lies have you told?

Or were you waiting
For my secrets
To unfold?
I think this may be true.
Some boys do.

And you'd say you won't
But I knew you might
Some time at night
When the time was right,
The moon was full
And the room was silent
And empty.
Stolen glances from
A cluster of friends.
Stolen kisses
In parking lots.

As they who came
Before you.

The liar.
The thief.
The thug.
The jock.
The jerk.
The poet.
The addict.
The rock.
The player.
The strayer.
The innocent
Boys that do.

The dark knight.
The golden boy.
The martyr.
The sadist.
The priest.

But what is love,
I ponder,
Swearing I never will.
But I will
Because I want more.
Too much.

And now,
Here you are
High on a scaffold,
Mourning your sexual awakening.

Tell absolutely no one.
Of course,
I wouldn't dare.

Step into my confessional
And let me
Punish you because
You've been so bad.
Think about
All the dirty things
And naughty dreams
You've had.
Let's make them
Come true.

For, the only true sin
Is to not believe in me
And to not believe in you.

Drink a cup
Of my absolution.
It's my solution
To the sin of your guilt.

If I fall,
Will you catch me?
I will catch you
If you fall.

Because some boys do
And some boys don't
Others will
While others won't,
And we all make
This world go round together.

The lines are
Grayer now.
I don't know
What is reality
And what is fantasy—
Which boys don't
And which boys do.

And you…
Don't take too long
With simple choices.

I'm listening hard
For the pining voices
Of the boys that do.

I Never Had the Chance to Say Good-Bye

Dance with me one last time
And pretend that you are mine
Because I was always yours.
Then, when you pray to God tonight
See my heart and lonely place
I never said it to your face
I love you,
And I never had the chance to say good-bye.

You said my name
So richly, deeply, thickly
With the curve of your European tongue
And made me feel I was the one
Then danced me down this long regret
And became a man I shan't forget
But I never had the chance to say good-bye.

You told me not to love you.
You warned me it would hurt.
I should have heeded
Those words of wisdom.
It's too late,
For now, I live them.
I'm torn and battered
Burned and broken
Keep my heartache as a token.
I never had the chance to say good-bye.

As they say, I've let you go.
So, end this game and come back home
So I'll know
You meant to say the things you said
When I took you to my bed.
You wrapped me up in arms of might
Like my angel, through the night
Kissed me softly as you held me
And then, I never had the chance to say good-bye.

Now, trapped in your convent
Filled with men
Please remember then
When we laughed, cried, birthed, died.
When they ask me to smile,
I say I'm happy
But, I cry.
If they ask you all about me,
I'll bet you lie.
Still, we never had the chance to say
Good-bye.